Fantastic Cats

Bengal

Sierra Wilson

AV2

www.openlightbox.com

Step 1
Go to www.openlightbox.com

Step 2
Enter this unique code

BNPCWJDRZ

Step 3
Explore your interactive eBook!

AV2 is optimized for use on any device

Your interactive eBook comes with...

Contents
Browse a live contents page to easily navigate through resources

Audio
Listen to sections of the book read aloud

Videos
Watch informative video clips

Weblinks
Gain additional information for research

Slideshows
View images and captions

Try This!
Complete activities and hands-on experiments

Key Words
Study vocabulary, and complete a matching word activity

Quizzes
Test your knowledge

Share
Share titles within your Learning Management System (LMS) or Library Circulation System

Citation
Create bibliographical references following the Chicago Manual of Style

This title is part of our AV2 digital subscription

1-Year K–5 Subscription
ISBN 978-1-7911-3320-7

Access hundreds of AV2 titles with our digital subscription.
Sign up for a FREE trial at www.openlightbox.com/trial

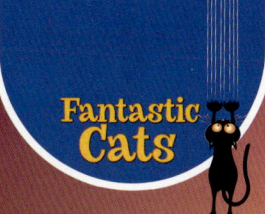

Bengal

Contents

AV2 Book Code 2
Name the Cat 4
Meet the Bengal 6
Bengal History 8
Striking Spots and Patterns 10
Active Friends 12
Endless Energy 14
Caring for Your Bengal 16
Healthy Bengals 18
If You Like Bengal Cats 20
Bengal Quiz 22
Key Words/Index 23

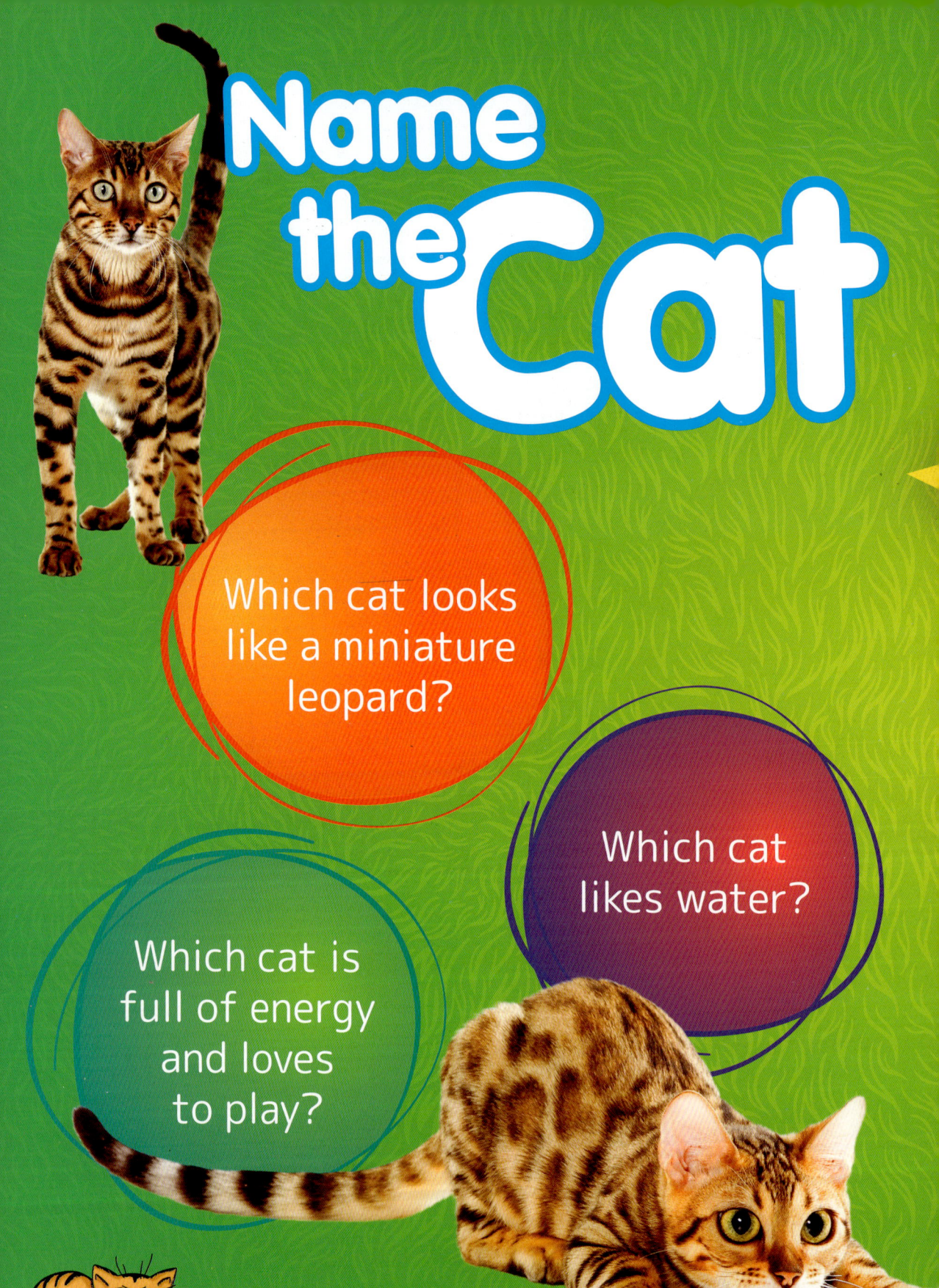

Name the Cat

Which cat looks like a miniature leopard?

Which cat likes water?

Which cat is full of energy and loves to play?

Meet the Bengal

With their eye-catching fur patterns, Bengal cats are easy to spot. At first glance, they might look like wild cats, but they are true house cats on the inside. These cats are friendly and loving toward their owners. Bengals can provide their families with plenty of entertainment. They are smart, curious, and love to play and explore. They even like to play in the water. Bengal cats are often beloved house pets, and many also take part in cat shows.

Bengals are a fairly new **breed**, but they have grown quickly in popularity around the world. Celebrities including actress Kristen Stewart, comedian Jerry Seinfeld, and singer Bruce Springsteen have Bengal cats. This has helped to make the Bengal breed renowned.

The Bengal Breed

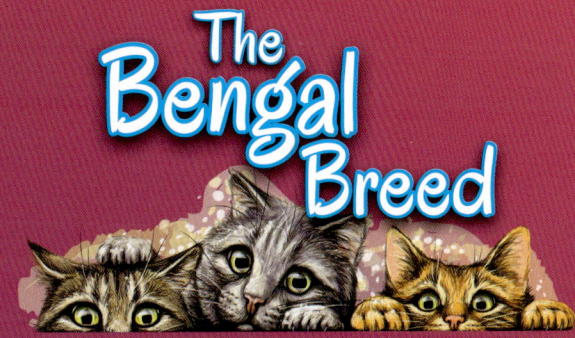

Until the 1970s, Bengals were known as **"safari cats"**

Bengal kittens usually go to their new homes when they are **12** to **16 weeks** old.

Bengals can weigh up to **15 pounds** (7 kilograms).

Bengal History

In 1963, a woman named Jean Mill developed the Bengal breed in California. Her goal was to create a new **domestic** cat breed with the look of a wild cat. She began by crossing a black domestic cat with an undomesticated **species**, the Asian leopard cat.

Creating a house cat breed from an undomesticated breed takes many years. **Breeders** need to make sure that the new kittens will be gentle and safe to have as pets. To help the breed succeed, Mill asked Dr. Willard Centerwall, a **genetics** expert, for help. Dr. Centerwall provided Mill with female cats to breed. In 1985, the Bengal breed was first presented at a cat show. The same year, Mill sold Bengal kittens for the first time. Over the years, the breed became more and more popular. It was officially recognized by the Cat Fanciers' Association (CFA), an important **pedigree registry**, in 2016.

Bangladesh

Bengals get their unique appearance from Asian leopard cats. These small felines are found throughout many Asian countries, including Bangladesh. Leopard cats can survive in many **habitats**, such as forests and mountain areas.

Striking Spots and Patterns

Bengals stand out with their exotic appearance. Although they come in different colors and patterns, all Bengals have dark markings that match those of their Asian leopard cat **ancestors**.

SPOTS
A Bengal's coat is patterned with a blend of spots and stripes. The cat's leopard-like spots are called rosettes.

FUR
Bengals have **dense** fur that is as soft as that of a rabbit. Their fur comes in three main colors. These are brown, silver, and snow.

LEGS
Bengals have longer hind legs than front legs. They have a graceful walk and are powerful jumpers.

NOSE
Bengal noses are wide, with a leather-like appearance.

EYES
Bengals have large, oval eyes that come in many colors, including green, yellow, gold, blue, and aqua.

Active Friends

Bengal cats are known for their loving personalities. They get along well with children, as well as dogs, and other cats. However, owning a Bengal along with small pets such as fish or rodents can be a challenge. Bengals have a strong hunting **instinct** that can put small pets at risk.

Bengals are smart and curious, and have **dexterous** paws. They can figure out complicated tasks, such as turning light switches on and off or opening kitchen cabinets to explore inside. Bengal cats can also be trained to do tricks. They might be trained with a **clicker** to perform different tricks when they hear a clicking sound. Bengal cats are very "talkative." They do not just make regular "meow" sounds. They also chirp, trill, and yowl.

Endless Energy

Bengal cats are intelligent and energetic. To live happy, healthy lives, they need plenty of play and exercise. Bengals love to climb. They enjoy sitting in high places and using climbing structures, such as cat trees.

Bengals also enjoy playing games with their owners. They can learn to fetch and "chase the light" with a laser pointer. Cat toys help keep Bengal cats happy and engaged. Some toys that work well include puzzle toys, table tennis balls, and bags or boxes that can be used as hiding places. Unlike most house cats, Bengals like water and may enjoy playing in a bathtub or with a small fountain.

If Bengal cats become too bored, they sometimes get into trouble. They might scratch the furniture or cause a mess. With proper attention, opportunities for play, and training, owners can avoid these unwelcome **behaviors**.

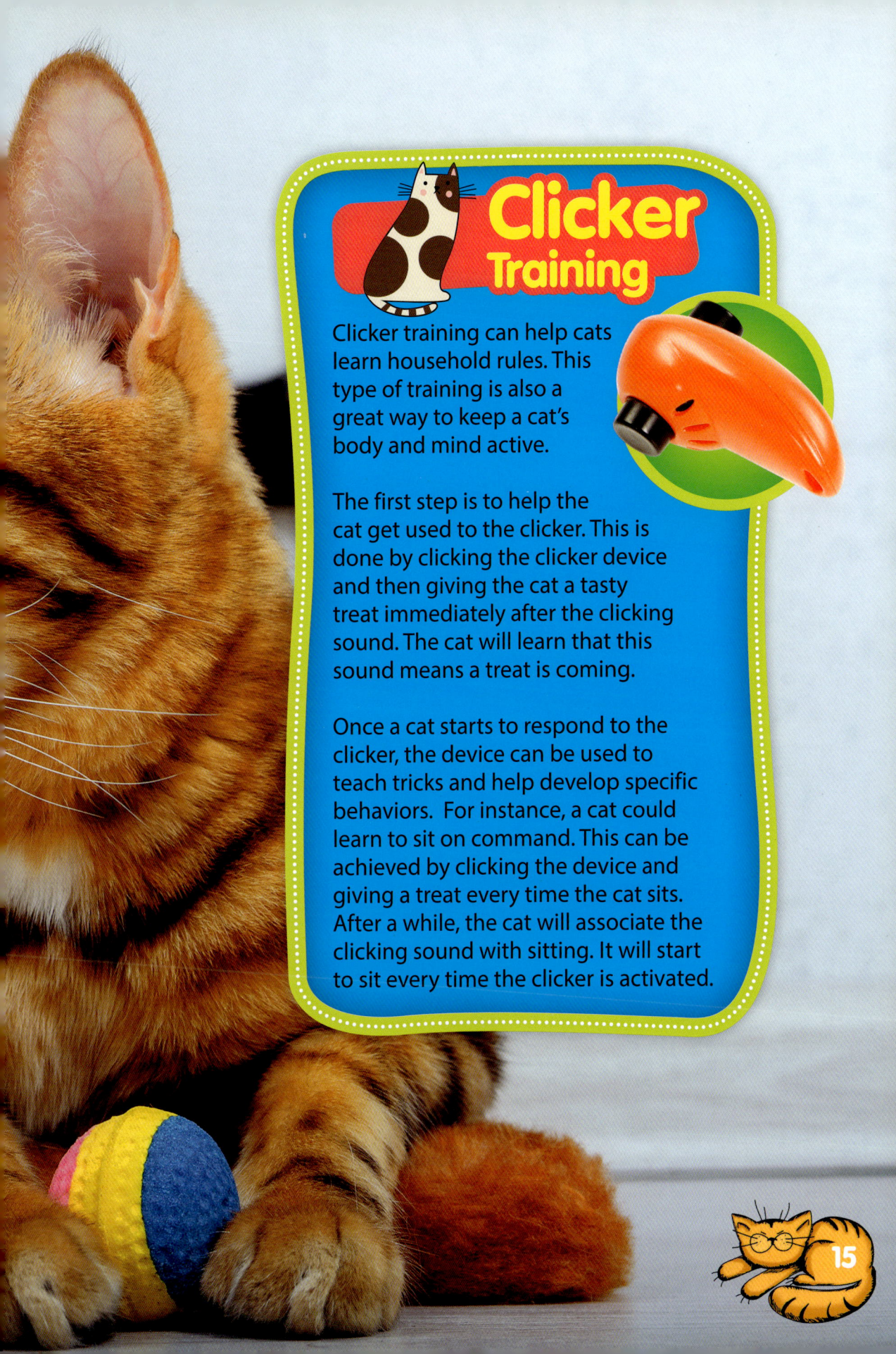

Clicker Training

Clicker training can help cats learn household rules. This type of training is also a great way to keep a cat's body and mind active.

The first step is to help the cat get used to the clicker. This is done by clicking the clicker device and then giving the cat a tasty treat immediately after the clicking sound. The cat will learn that this sound means a treat is coming.

Once a cat starts to respond to the clicker, the device can be used to teach tricks and help develop specific behaviors. For instance, a cat could learn to sit on command. This can be achieved by clicking the device and giving a treat every time the cat sits. After a while, the cat will associate the clicking sound with sitting. It will start to sit every time the clicker is activated.

Caring for Your Bengal

Bengal cats have short fur and do not shed very much. This makes their coats fairly easy to care for. Short coats also make Bengals one of the best cat breed choices for people with **allergies**. These cats groom their own fur well. However, brushing a Bengal once per week can keep its fur shiny and help avoid **hairballs**. Due to their love of water, Bengals can also be bathed if they become especially dirty.

Bengals should have their teeth brushed regularly. They should also have their claws trimmed every couple of weeks. Trimming a Bengal's claws makes playing safer for adults and children alike. It can also help curb the cat's natural scratching instinct.

Cat Supplies

Cat Fountain Fountains with filters give cats safe and fresh water to drink. A fountain allows Bengals to drink plenty of water and gives them a fun place to play, too.

Scratching Post Cats are naturally inclined to scratch things. A scratching post provides Bengals and other cats with an appropriate place to satisfy their scratching urge.

Cat Tree Cats use cat trees for climbing, scratching, and resting up high. One or more cat trees with multiple platforms can help keep Bengals entertained.

Litter Box Like all cats, Bengals need a clean litter box to avoid accidents and dirtiness in the house. If a litter box is dirty, cats may refuse to use it.

Healthy Bengals

Bengals are athletic and strong, with sturdy muscles. They can be fed regular cat food without problems. However, some owners like to feed their Bengals raw food or put them on no-grain diets.

Bengals should see a **veterinarian** regularly to receive routine **vaccinations**. A vet can also address any health concerns and give advice on proper care. Bengal cats may be susceptible to certain diseases. While their Asian leopard cat ancestors are **immune** to the virus that causes feline leukemia, Bengals are not. They can also develop heart and eye conditions. Responsible cat breeders can take steps to breed kittens who have a lower risk for many of these health issues.

Life Span of Pet Cats

Life Span	Breed
8–14 Years	Manx
9–15 Years	Abyssinian
12–15 Years	Egyptian Mau
12–16 Years	Bengal
15–20 Years	Siamese

If You Like Bengal Cats...

Some people love Bengals for their leopard-like appearance. Others enjoy them for their energy or sweet personalities. If you like Bengal cats, here are some similar cats you might also appreciate.

Chausie

The Chausie is another breed created from a mix between a house cat and an undomesticated species, the jungle cat. Chausies are strong and active. They can develop close bonds with their owners.

Egyptian Mau

Much like Bengals, Egyptian Maus have spotted fur and an exotic appearance. These cats are smart, active, and loyal. They are the fastest house cat breed and can run at speeds up to 30 miles (48 km) per hour.

Korat

Korats are very smart. Like Bengals, these cats can easily learn tricks and enjoy playing with toys. However, Korats also enjoy some quiet time. They have sweet and calm personalities.

Savannah

Savannah cats are a cross between house cats and servals, felines that live on the African savanna. Savannahs have long, graceful necks and spotted fur. These cats are playful and active. They share a love of water with Bengals.

Siamese

The Siamese is one of the most well-known cat breeds. Siamese cats are highly intelligent, just like Bengals. These cats are curious and full of energy. They love attention and can be loud "talkers."

Bengal Quiz

1 Which cat breed can run up to 30 miles (48 km) per hour?

2 What is the lifespan of a Bengal?

3 To which disease is the Asian leopard cat immune?

4 How often should a Bengal's fur be brushed?

5 Which tool can be used to train Bengals to do tricks?

6 What are servals?

7 Who developed the Bengal breed?

8 How much do Bengal cats weigh?

Answers: 1. Egyptian Mau 2. 12-16 years 3. Feline leukemia 4. Once per week 5. A clicker 6. Felines that live on the African savanna 7. Jean Mill 8. Up to 15 pounds (7 kg)

Key Words

allergies: sensitivities to different substances that may cause adverse reactions in the body
ancestors: ancient animals or plants from which other animals or plants have evolved
behaviors: specific actions
breed: a group of animals with similar appearances belonging to the same species
breeders: people who raise and sell baby animals
clicker: a small device with a button that makes a clicking sound when pressed
dense: thick
dexterous: skilled at moving
domestic: able to live alongside humans
genetics: the study of how characteristics are passed down in living things
habitats: the environments where certain animals can be found in nature
hairballs: balls of hair that may form inside a cat's stomach
immune: having a strong resistance to a certain disease
instinct: a natural behavior with which animals are born
pedigree registry: an organization in charge of certifying that individual animals belong to a specific breed
species: animals or plants that share certain features and can reproduce together
vaccinations: medical treatments to produce immunity against specific diseases
veterinarian: a doctor for animals

Index

Abyssinian 19
Asian leopard cat 8, 9, 10, 18, 22

Bengal 19

cat fountain 14, 17
cat trees 14, 17
Centerwall, Willard 8
Chausie 20
clicker 13, 15, 22

Egyptian Mau 19, 20, 22
eyes 11, 18

feline leukemia 18, 22
fur 6, 10, 16, 20, 21, 22

Korat 21

legs 11
litter box 17

Manx 19
Mill, Jean 8, 22

Savannah 21
scratching post 17
Siamese 19, 21
spots 10, 20, 21

toys 14, 21

Get the best of both worlds.

AV2 bridges the gap between print and digital.

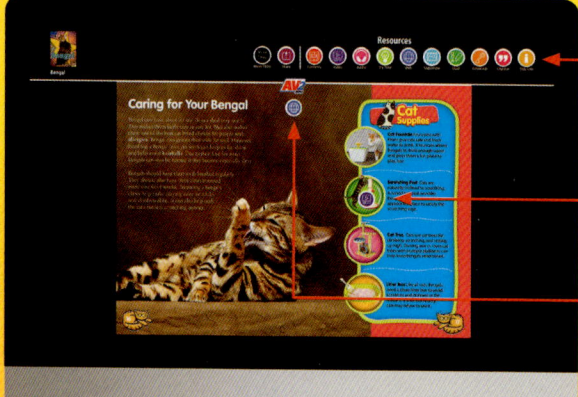

The expandable resources toolbar enables quick access to content including **videos**, **audio**, **activities**, **weblinks**, **slideshows**, **quizzes**, and **key words**.

Animated videos make static images come alive.

Resource icons on each page help readers to further **explore key concepts**.

Published by Lightbox Learning Inc.
276 5th Avenue
Suite 704 #917
New York, NY 10001
Website: www.openlightbox.com

Copyright ©2023 Lightbox Learning Inc.
All rights reserved. No part of this publication may be reproduced, stored in a retrieval system, or transmitted in any form or by any means, electronic, mechanical, photocopying, recording, or otherwise, without the prior written permission of the publisher.

Library of Congress Cataloging-in-Publication Data

Names: Wilson, Sierra, author.
Title: Bengal / Sierra Wilson.
Description: New York, NY : Lightbox Learning Inc., [2023] | Series:
  Fantastic cats | Includes index. | Audience: Grades 2-3
Identifiers: LCCN 2022012032 (print) | LCCN 2022012033 (ebook) | ISBN
  9781791149178 (library binding) | ISBN 9781791149185 (library binding) |
  ISBN 9781791149192 (ebook other) Subjects: LCSH: Bengal cat--Juvenile literature.
Classification: LCC SF449.B45 W55 2023 (print) | LCC SF449.B45 (ebook) | DDC 636.8/22--dc23/eng/20220413
LC record available at https://lccn.loc.gov/2022012032
LC ebook record available at https://lccn.loc.gov/2022012033

Printed in Guangzhou, China
1 2 3 4 5 6 7 8 9 0 26 25 24 23 22

052022
101121

Project Coordinator: Sara Cucini
Designer: Terry Paulhus

Photo Credits
Every reasonable effort has been made to trace ownership and to obtain permission to reprint copyright material. The publisher would be pleased to have any errors or omissions brought to its attention so that they may be corrected in subsequent printings. The publisher acknowledges Alamy, Getty Images, Minden, and Shutterstock as its primary image suppliers for this title.

View new titles and product videos at www.openlightbox.com